MAKERSPACES™

GETTING THE MOST OUT OF
MAKERSPACES
TO BUILD
UNMANNED
AERIAL
VEHICLES

DON RAUF

Published in 2015 by The Rosen Publishing Group, Inc.
29 East 21st Street, New York, NY 10010

Copyright © 2015 by The Rosen Publishing Group, Inc.

First Edition

Library of Congress Cataloging-in-Publication Data

Rauf, Don.
Getting the most out of makerspaces to build unmanned aerial vehicles/Don Rauf.
   pages cm.—(Makerspaces)
Audience: Grades 5–8.
Includes bibliographical references and index.
ISBN 978-1-4777-7827-2 (library bound)—ISBN 978-1-4777-7829-6 (pbk.)—
ISBN 978-1-4777-7830-2 (6-pack)
1. Airplanes—Models—Radio control—Juvenile literature. 2. Drone aircraft—Juvenile literature. 3. Micro air vehicles—Juvenile literature. I. Title.
TL770.R36 2015
629.133—dc23
                                                                          2014003085

Manufactured in the United States of America

CONTENTS

Makerspaces provide a comfortable, roomy environment where young people can create. Groups often gather in these spaces to build technology-based projects such as unmanned aerial vehicles.

Makerspaces are both spaces and community groups where ideas can take flight. Literally. The maker movement is bringing people together in makerspaces to do hands-on creative and often technology-oriented projects, including building small model aircraft. One of the most popular types of makerspace projects is constructing unmanned aerial vehicles (UAVs).

Makerspaces are also teaching people to build robots, fix bicycles, program gadgets, use 3-D printers, and more. Makerspaces are all about bringing people together so they can learn how to do things that may at first seem beyond their grasp. They often take place in libraries, schools, and community centers, where people can participate, collaborate, and explore.

Makers are artists, hobbyists, enthusiasts and students or amateurs interested in innovation, creating new products and producing value in the community. With the help of pooling talent and volunteer experts in a makerspace, a young person can come up with an idea and bring that vision to life. Some makers go on to become entrepreneurs and start companies. Other makers are laying the foundation to become tomorrow's engineers. And that's a valuable skill.

Makers make comics, games, clothes, robots, UAVs, and many other items. The term "makerspace" originated around 2005 when *Make* magazine began publishing. Makerspace.com was registered in 2011 and the term really took off. While *Make* magazine has certainly played a role in the maker phenomenon, the movement goes beyond that. The term "maker" is not owned by *Make* magazine or any one entity. It simply captures the whole spirit of do-it-yourself construction, design, and engineering.

Maker Faires have also contributed to the maker movement. The first one launched in 2006 in the Bay Area in California and Maker Faires have been held in more and more cities since then. These are gatherings of tech enthusiasts, crafters, educators, tinkerers, hobbyists, engineers, science clubs, authors, artists, students, and commercial exhibitors, who all come together at a Maker Faire to show what they have made and to share what they have learned.

Makerspaces are springing up around the country, so get online, do some searching, and see if there's one near you or a part of your school. Makerspaces can spark a person's sense of creativity and innovation and show that things that seem impossible to do can come to life. As Steve Jobs, the founder of Apple computers, once said, "Let's go invent tomorrow." And a makerspace may be just the place for you to do that.

CHAPTER ONE

WHAT ARE UNMANNED AERIAL VEHICLES?

Look up in the sky! It's a bird! It's a plane! It's an unmanned aerial vehicle. Although not everyone has heard the term "unmanned aerial vehicle" (UAV), many people are familiar with the word "drone." These aircraft have no pilots or passengers. They are either guided by a controller from the ground or directed by a program that is installed on the aircraft.

Although they vary in size, UAVs are, in general, all much lighter and smaller than standard aircraft. The Predator, which is a type of UAV used by the United States Air Force, is 27 feet (8.2 m) long with a 49-foot (14.9-m) wingspan. Compare that to your standard 747 commercial jet, which has a wingspan of 195 feet (59.4 m) and a length of 250 feet (76.2 m). For a hobbyist who wants to make a drone at home, a UAV can be just a little under 2 feet (0.6 m) long and weigh 4 pounds (1.8 kg).

In many ways, unmanned aerial vehicles are the same as radio-controlled (RC) model planes that hobbyists build and fly. The line separating the two is virtually nonexistent. There are some differences, though. In general, the user of a

University of Missouri students guide a quadcopter drone off the ground at Columbia's Hinkson Field. Quadcopters are popular projects among maker groups.

radio-controlled plane can always see the aircraft from the ground. The pilot guides the aircraft through a handheld radio transmitter that communicates with a receiver inside the small flying machine. While a UAV can be this, it can also be equipped with a computer, a camera, and other remote sensing equipment, which lets it run on autopilot.

"Radio-controlled aircraft" is also a term that is used if the craft is exclusively for recreational purposes. UAVs are not only created by hobbyists and makers, they are also the un-piloted craft built by the military and businesses. "Drone" is typically the term used for a UAV that the government or military employs for a specific mission. However, the terms "RC aircraft," "UAV," and "drone" are often used interchangeably.

UAVS IN THE MODERN WORLD

Makers are interested in UAVs because they are being used more and more for many different purposes. Maker groups that build UAVs follow how they are being used in the real world, and some study the types of UAVs being developed by the military and other groups so they can make similar aircraft. Seeing real-world applications of UAVs inspires young makers.

The military and governments use drones to attack an enemy by dropping bombs and missiles from these unmanned aircraft. Drones can even be directed to assassinate

Although the UAV project Prime Air is in early development at Amazon, CEO Jeff Bezos envisions a world where drones can deliver packages in thirty minutes or less.

an enemy leader or terrorists. UAVs can also be flown on information-gathering missions, often recording images from hard-to-reach regions and relaying pictures and other data via satellite.

In recent years, UAVs have been increasingly used because they can be flown without causing physical harm to a pilot or crew, and they can be kept in the air for very long periods of time. The Zephyr is a British drone that can remain aloft for more than eighty-two hours nonstop. They are also more affordable to build than normal aircraft.

What Might Drones Do in the Future?

Makers are envisioning all sorts of purposes for UAVs. One makerspace group in the Bay Area in California conducted a robot-delivered cupcake contest with entries including UAVs. One group of makers has dedicated themselves to providing "long-endurance, mission-capable aircraft with the integrated pastry delivery systems required to deliver delicious cup-shaped pastries." Domino's Pizza envisions delivering pizzas via drones and they've tested the idea in Britain.

Amazon recently made headlines when its CEO Jeff Bezos announced that Amazon.com is testing delivering packages using drones. Bezos is exploring the idea that packages can be delivered more quickly via UAVs through a service with the working name of Prime Air. He said that UAVs have the potential to deliver packages in thirty minutes or less. Amazon has said that one day seeing UAVs zipping through the sky might be as common as seeing UPS and other delivery trucks bringing packages to homes and offices.

Nebraska University has a new Drone Journalism Lab in Lincoln that is developing journalism programs with the intent of gathering data, video, and other images from the air to help cover military missions and natural disasters when access is difficult or dangerous.

Drones have been in the news in recent times because the United States and Britain have used them on military missions in Afghanistan, Iraq, and Pakistan. For military use, drones generally require a few people to operate them. For example, for a mission in Iraq, a team may launch the drone in an area near the conflict. Via satellite, visual information may then be sent back to the United States. A "pilot" in Nevada may actually fly and steer the UAV in an Iraqi battle zone. Another person may operate monitors, cameras, and sensors from that Nevada base. Another expert may be in communication with leaders and troops in the war zones, relaying information from the drone to them.

FOR LAW ENFORCEMENT, SCIENCE, AND BEYOND

The FBI has been using drones for surveillance in the United States as well. FBI officials have said that drones are useful in hostage and barricade situations because they fly more quietly and are less visible than traditional aircraft, such as helicopters. The FBI has said that it used a UAV to monitor a situation where a boy was held hostage in a bunker in Alabama. Other law enforcement professionals see the potential to use drones to hunt for lost children, conduct search-and-rescue efforts, or possibly track or find criminals.

While UAVs can help in emergencies, criminal investigations, and saving lives, many people are concerned about the potential for spying and want to protect their privacy.

A maintenance crew prepares a Predator drone for a surveillance flight near the U.S.-Mexico border to search for drug smugglers and immigrants crossing illegally.

However, fans of unmanned aircraft point out that they have applications that go beyond law enforcement. UAVs may be used to study weather and for hurricane hunting, to track the course of wildfires, view traffic, map geography, and even fly over golf courses to see which fairways need to be watered.

Some makers want to emphasize the positive uses of UAVs. Recently, some makerspace groups have been getting involved with the Wildlife Conservation UAV Challenge. These groups are designing, building, and flying UAVs to combat wildlife poaching and illegal wildlife trafficking in Africa. The Drone User Network Group recently announced the Drone Social Impact Award, which will give $5,000 to someone who can document the most socially beneficial use of a drone for under $3,000.

CHAPTER TWO

BLAST OFF! ROCKETING INTO THE WORLD OF UAVs

Before making sophisticated remote controlled planes, young makers may find it helpful to start at a more simple level with some of the basics for making model airplanes and flight-related projects that teach the fundamentals of aerodynamics and design.

Model rockets are often a great starting point because model rocket groups are already established throughout the country. Model rockets are relatively simple to build, and they're literally a blast. Also, they may not be officially called UAVs, but rockets really could be considered a form of UAV because they are unmanned, they fly, and they are vehicles.

For years, the National Association of Rocketry and the Tripoli Rocketry Association have been educating people about how to make model rockets, and these are two organizations worth checking out for those who want to get involved in model rocketry.

Young Astronauts Club coordinator John Barfield *(left)* and fifth grader Chelsea Girard launch a model cruise missile as part of an end-of-year big blast.

For less than $50, a standard rocket-build kit can be purchased at a hobby shop. These types of kits make great makerspace projects. In a makerspace, fellow makers can share tips, help each other build, and encourage each other to complete their rockets. The kits generally include a rocket with parachute; an engine/motor, igniter, and wadding (a nonflammable filler material placed in a model rocket airframe to protect the parachute; a launch pad and stand; and a launch controller with cables. Launch controllers can provide a lesson in simple electronics. These devices supply power to an igniter, which fires the rocket engine.

Compressed air rockets are also popular to make among the maker crowd. Maker Shed advertises some kits, but they can be made from scratch with PVC pipe. They often involve a bicycle pump to supply the air pressure and an electric sprinkler valve to create the sudden release of pressure, which can send the rocket shooting toward the heavens. *Make* magazine gives information on how to create these unique "UAVs," and they recommend them because they are fast, easy-to-build, and can soar hundreds of feet into the sky.

Makershed.com, which features many projects for young makers, describes how to make the "rocket glider." This small model aircraft is even more affordable than a rocket, costing just $17. Glue, sandpaper, and a hobby knife are the only equipment needed.

Some makers make simple nonflying models of airplanes to get a sense of what aircraft is all about. In Westport, Connecticut, the public library celebrated the first year anniversary of its makerspace by displaying two 1930s GeeBee racer model airplanes, which were built in the makerspace and now hang from the ceiling. While the planes don't fly, their design and history have been an inspiration for young makers who are interested in aviation.

For those interested in creating a true unmanned aerial vehicle, building a rocket, launching a high-altitude balloon, making a glider, or constructing a model plane is a good place to begin and get a sense of aviation and aerodynamics.

SETTING UP A MAKERSPACE TO WORK ON UAV PROJECTS

For those who want to launch into a maker-based project involving UAVs or other flight-oriented craft, the workspace is essential. The first step to finding a workspace is to see if there is a makerspace near you. Libraries, universities, museums, science centers, and community organizations (such as 4-H clubs, YMCAs, YWCAs, Boy Scouts, Boys and Girls Clubs, and Girl Scouts) have all started makerspaces. In San Francisco, there is a project underway to establish a makerspace in a hospital where nurses and other staff members can test ideas and invent medical technologies and devices to improve the quality of care.

There may also be spaces that are not affiliated with any other organizations and are makerspaces in their own right. For example, Seattle has Maker Haus, Jigsaw Renaissance, and Matrix Create: Space, which are all dedicated to empowering makers to pursue their projects.

HIGH-FLYING HELLO KITTY

High-flying balloons are yet another way for young makers to explore the world of flight. Makerspace.com profiled young maker Lauren Rojas of Antioch, California. At age thirteen, Rojas decided to launch her Hello Kitty doll as high in the air as she could for a seventh grade science project. Using a special high altitude balloon and camera, Rojas was able to record Hello Kitty's high-flying adventure.

She bought the high-flying balloon kit from a company called High Altitude Science, which sells near space balloons that range in price from $60 to $400. The balloon, which rises when filled with helium, soared nearly 100,000 feet (30,480 m) into space. It flew through the coldest region of our planet's atmosphere. It traveled across the boundary layer between the troposphere and the stratosphere known as the tropopause.

After about a two-hour journey to the edge of space, the balloon burst but a parachute then deployed, which keeps the payload from falling too fast. The payload is basically the housing that can hold a GPS satellite tracker, a camera, any other scientific equipment, and other materials that the user wants to send into near space.

For a seventh grade science class, Lauren Rojas made a do-it-yourself high-flying balloon craft and sent her Hello Kitty soaring to the edge of outer space and safely back to earth.

Some makerspaces are equipped with state-of-the-art technology: 3D printers, vinyl cutters, soldering equipment, electronics, and fabrication equipment for working with various metals, plastic, and other materials.

Makerspaces to create UAVs and other devices need to provide roomy worktables and lots of light. They also should be equipped with the tools and supplies needed to build. That's why technical and vocational classrooms at some schools have been transformed into makerspaces. Many schools now offer extracurricular programs in building robotics and in some ways a UAV can be seen as a flying robot. Like a robot, it can be guided and manipulated remotely. A school may already have a space dedicated to robotics and that may be well-suited for a UAV makerspace as well.

The Makerspace.com website provides a manual called *The Makerspace Playbook*, which gives recommendations to help anyone set up an effective makerspace or improve the workspace they currently have for UAV projects or other endeavors. In general, having these tools on hand in a makerspace can help to build a UAV. Some crucial items are wire cutters, wire strippers, hammers, strong glue (possibly a glue gun), screwdrivers (of various sizes), and a soldering iron and solder.

Making can potentially involve a certain amount of cutting, stripping wire, sawing, hammering, and using electricity and heat for something like soldering. Makers have to work with care to not harm themselves or others. Always have an adult nearby, a first aid kit on the premises that is readily accessible, and a means to call 911 in case of emergencies.

CHAPTER THREE

BUILDING BLOCKS FOR A MAKERSPACE UAV PROJECT

As the makerspace manager at the Grand Center Arts Academy in St. Louis, Missouri, Andrew Goodin is a big supporter of the maker movement. His makerspace is a collaborative workshop where students use their artistic abilities to solve real-world problems in science, technology, engineering, and mathematics. The makerspace here helps creative students who are involved with theater, visual arts, dance, and music combine their talents with projects that have a base in science, technology, math, and engineering. Goodin has seen the potential in makerspaces to develop valuable workplace skills and to direct student attention toward something productive, which can even help curb school bullying.

One of the projects Goodin planned was to have his students build a type of unmanned aerial vehicle called a quadcopter. Quadcopters are very popular in the maker universe right now. Goodin has inspired his students to take on the project by showing them how the modern technology of UAVs is being used for surveying disaster areas and other humanitarian efforts. Plus, it's fun to build something that flies.

Google Glass eyewear can be used to control drones, as seen here at NodeCopter, an event where people come to program toy drones.

The goal of the project is to teach three major areas of technology—3-D modeling, circuitry, and computer programming—in an authentic project-based application. The first step will involve students working on 3-D modeling to create the UAV frame. Specialized computer graphics software allows students to build a wireframe model that represents the object to be built. The computer modeling involves different types of geometric data such as shapes, lines, and curved surfaces.

Three-dimensional modeling has many real-world applications. In the computer gaming industry, it is used to create realistic-looking characters and landscapes. In the health care field, computer modeling has been used to make models of organs for medical study. Two popular 3-D software programs are Maya and 3DS Max.

After modeling, students will go on to learn, plan, construct, and wire the circuitry that powers the motors, which

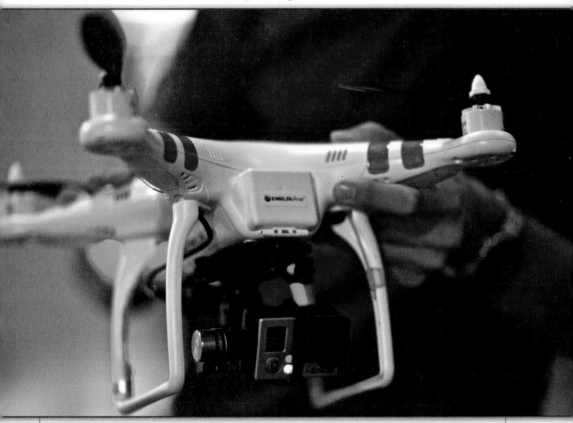

This Phantom drone comes equipped with a Hero Pro camera. The camera can be controlled by an operator on the ground and capture images as it flies.

will keep the UAV in the air. The circuitry is a detailed plan of all the electrical components required to operate the aircraft—to control direction, lift, and other functions.

Finally, students will learn to operate the UAV with a remote control, but they will also learn how to program a small computer that will put the aircraft on autopilot so it can run a flight pattern without anyone "piloting" it from the ground. The ultimate goal for Goodin and his students is to have the aircraft run an obstacle course by following a computer program.

MATERIALS NEEDED FOR A UAV

Raising funds for materials can be a struggle for many makerspace groups. Goodin reached out for funding through a crowdfunding website designed for teachers called DonorsChoose.org. His project shows the supplies and other elements that are needed for the typical makerspace UAV project.

A look at the supply list below gives some idea of some of the materials that makers need to get started on constructing a UAV.

• Wire especially made for servos (little motors).
• Silicone wire, which is really silicone-coated copper wire used for electronics projects.
• Plane glue.
• Wattmeter and power analyzer, to measure electrical power.
• Propeller balancer, a device used to balance aircraft propellers. An unbalanced propeller may cause damage to the engine

or aircraft frame and that could lead to a crash. An out-of-balance propeller will cause an aircraft to vibrate and be hard to control. An unbalanced propeller could break during use.

• Cable sleeve tubing to basically keep wiring neat, together, and protected.

• Transmitter and receiving system.

• Battery.

• Motors.

• Propellers.

• Ardupilot Mega, a relatively inexpensive microcontroller ($159 to $240 with a GPS [global positioning system]) to enhance traditional remote control aircraft. The Ardupilot can improve performance of a piloted airplane and create a fully-autonomous aircraft that can fly missions on its own.

CONTROLLING A UAV WITH ARDUPILOT

To control a UAV, many makers will use Ardupilot. Ardupilot uses open-source (free and changeable) Arduino hardware and software. Arduino has built a name for itself by making easy-to-use and program small computers (powered by microcontrollers) that can operate devices and gadgets. Students have used Arduino to build robots that sense heat and can blow out a candle and door locks that open only when a specific pattern is rapped on the door.

With the Ardupilot aboard the UAV, mission control can communicate with and operate motors, wiring, and telemetry.

LET'S THROW IN THE "TOWEL"

While UAV projects can get fairly complicated and involved, some do-it-yourself projects for building remote controlled aircraft are fairly simple. The Towel is a model radio controlled aircraft that has gotten a lot of attention in the maker world because it is easy to put together (an afternoon is all that's required) and it's inexpensive (about $100 worth of supplies).

Developed by the Brooklyn Aerodrome, this UAV design is basically constructed from a polystyrene insulation board with a reinforced area to host the electronics and motor. It's known to be super easy to maneuver, it can land in a tight spot, and it can carry a camera.

Telemetry is the science and technology of automatic measurement and transmission of data by wire, radio, or other means from remote sources. The Ardupilot can also work along with a GPS to fly to specific locations. In addition, the Ardupilot can connect to a small onboard camera, which can transmit images back to the ground pilot.

CHAPTER FOUR

THE INNOVATION OF QUADCOPTERS

While many people think of UAVs as airplanes, makers have been building a new type of flying machine called the quadcopter (sometimes called a quadrocopter). In fact, quadcopters are all the rage in the maker world. If you go online, you'll see that there are many makerspaces across the country seeking funds to support their quadcopter projects.

The quadcopter places four propellers in a cross formation and rises into the air like a helicopter. They are classified as rotorcraft rather than fixed-wing aircraft, like a typical airplane. Quadcopters are the flying machines that Amazon.com CEO Jeff Bezos envisions filling the skies to deliver books and other goods to consumer doorsteps.

Why not just build a mini-helicopter? Unlike helicopters, quadcopters don't require the mechanical link needed to tilt the blade and change direction, which can make it easier to construct. Design and maintenance are easier as well.

"QUADCOPTERS" KEEP IMPROVING

Today, technology for quadcopters seems to be advancing rapidly. Quadcopters are admired for being stable, reliable,

Some of today's quadcopters, such as the AR. Drone, can be controlled with a smartphone or tablet computer.

and easy to control. One issue has been that if any one of the four blades stops spinning, the UAV would be sent crashing to the ground. Scientists have recently come up with solutions to prevent this. In this case, a small computer aboard the copters triggers the other three blades to adapt to the missing fourth and keep the vehicle airborne.

The maker attitude is to explore, modify, and get creative. Students have been exploring ways to modify the standard design of quadcopters. Students at ETH Zurich University have put together a combination quad/blimp. Called Project Skye, the flying contraption rises when filled with helium but has directional control.

The GRASP Lab out of the University of Pennsylvania has shown how multiple quadcopters can perform teamwork assignments. Equipped with clawlike grippers, a pack of small quadcopters can descend on heavy beams of wood, pick them up, and deliver them to a nearby location.

CHALLENGING BUT NOT DIFFICULT

While building a quadcopter can be time-consuming and require careful organization and brain power, constructing one does not have to cause frustration. On the Instructables.com website, one maker shows how he built a quadcopter in under an hour to win a bet. This individual used fir wood for the arms and plywood for the body. Using this framework, he added motors, motor controllers, batteries, and other components, along with the Ardupilot Mega flight controller, to quickly assemble a quadcopter.

Makers may also want to check out Oddcopter.com, which gives instructions on how to build a solid quad, easily and for around $200. The site shows how it is possible to build one without soldering (although soldering has its advantages

The Smallest and the Biggest UAVs

Imagine a soldier captured behind enemy lines. If he can't transmit a message via cell phone technology, he may be able to reach in his pocket, open a small container, and send off a tiny UAV that had been hidden there. Or the soldier could send the super-small UAV on a flight mission to an enemy camp to photograph top secret ground layouts or plans.

Researchers at the University of Oklahoma have been developing just such a device, which has a tubular shape and look that is remarkably like a cigarette. Students at the University of Oklahoma are also working on a UAV that can stay in flight for up to five years. Israel has produced what may be the biggest UAV. Called the Eitan, this UAV is about the size of a Boeing 737 airliner. It can stay aloft for twenty hours and has a maximum altitude of 40,000 feet (12,192 m). The Eitan can carry hundreds of pounds of equipment, which makes it ideal for delivering military supplies, weapons, and other equipment.

in terms of durability). The radio transmitter/receiver is simple and the long-lasting battery allows for long flight times.

In true maker spirit, one high school student online explained how to build a quadcopter from recycled and reused materials. Many materials that are discarded in the trash are strong, durable, and light enough for flight. A foam cup holder became the protective casing for sensitive electronic

New 3-D printers are allowing makers to produce their own components to build UAVs, such as this 3-D-printed quadcopter on display at the 3D Print UK studio in London.

equipment. Worn out pens and markers were emptied, taken apart, and put to use as spacers, or tubing for wires and screws. An old plastic food storage container not only became the base, but this material was used as a cover plate for the power board. Old PVC pipe, discarded from a home plumbing project, found new life as part of the arm and motor platform. The young maker also used recycled ice tea bottles, a peanut butter container, and pickle jar lids.

Students at Queen Mary University in London, featured on the *Make* website, have demonstrated that quadcopters can also be fueled by solar power. Running off the energy of the sun, the UAVs have the potential to travel great distances without having to return to mission control for battery replacement or refueling.

Some makerspace groups are putting modern 3-D printing technology to use building their quadcopters. The Midsouth Makers, for example, have a 3-D printer at their Memphis Makerspace. The 3-D printer can take a model and construct a frame for a quadcopter by building it one layer of material (such as plastic or metal) at a time, driven by computer-aided design (CAD) drawings.

One of the exciting things about UAVs is that they can be equipped with cameras that can transmit images back to the operator showing what the UAV sees. The technology is called first-person view (FPV) piloting. Also called remote-person view (RPV), the technique involves mounting a small video camera and analog television transmitter on a radio controlled aircraft and flying by means of a live video downlink, commonly displayed on video goggles or a portable LCD screen.

The monitors or screens for FPV are typically small and mounted on a tripod or in a briefcase shell. Modern monitor goggles are now available that basically put the image of the plane's field of view right in front of the ground pilot. Without FPV, a UAV operator would have to see the aircraft in the sky to control it and know where it is going. But with an FPV camera aboard, a maker can send his or her aircraft well beyond the field of view, guiding it via the transmitted images. The range of the UAV is only limited by the range of the transmitter.

HOW PEOPLE ARE USING FPV

Makerspace FPV-based projects are usually for pleasure viewing but they can have practical purposes. These purposes include surveying farmland to check on crops, viewing real estate developments and construction sites, finding illegal marijuana fields, inspecting miles of pipeline, checking on traffic, tracking tornados, spotting forest fires, documenting the beauty of nature and wildlife, and making aerial shots for Hollywood movies and sporting events.

The Federal Aviation Administration (FAA) and other organizations, however, are concerned about people using the cameras aboard FPVs for spying purposes, and regulations are being considered to control their use. Still, many businesses are springing up based on the new technology. ImageMark Strategy and Design launched a drone-powered aerial photo and video service for its clients, which include universities, golf resorts, and real estate firms.

A POPULAR ADDITION

FPV technology only became popular with makers at the end of the first decade of the 2000s. For makers, it is one

UAVs equipped with cameras have many uses, including filming athletes and fast-paced sporting events. Canada's Erik Guay is seen here competing in the FIS World Cup men's downhill skiing competition.

of the most popular additions when building UAVs. The Pandora Benevolent Society conducts makerspace workshops and presentations on how to create FPV flying robots using commercially-available kits and components. On the official *Make* website, scores of FPV examples are shown, including a prototype display unit by a maker in France that gives useful

Eirik Solheim flies a tiny quadcopter using first-person view (FPV), also known as remote-person view (RPV) at the Drones and Aerial Robotics Conference (DARC) in New York City.

information about flight, navigation, and power on the screen that the operator is viewing.

Recently, makers from all around the world gathered at the first ever Drone and Aerial Robotics Conference (DARC) in New York City. A demonstration here by the Norwegian Broadcasting Corporation involved flying a small, lightweight quadcopter out the stages' backdoor, directing it through several halls and passageways, and then returning it to the stage—all guided by FPV technology and costing just $169.

CAMERAS AND ANTENNAS MAKE A DIFFERENCE

A complete UAV kit with FPV capabilities can be purchased for about $128. For makerspace FPV projects, GoPro brand cameras are popular because they are small, light, and powerful. A small data card in the camera can record all the visual data and then the pilot can remove the card and download the flight video onto a computer. The GoPro now comes with an app that allows it to transmit images to a smartphone. Maker groups are considering how to use this in piloting their UAVs. Using the latest technology and software, makers can also rig their FPV gear so it records onto a laptop or notebook.

Those in a makerspace group who want to get the best performance from FPV have to consider the camera they are using and the antenna. Makers may shop around for cameras that work best under different lighting conditions. Often, the operators will want to fly at dusk when visibility can be difficult, so high resolution, black light compensation, and color saturation are important.

Antennas are a critical link between UAVs and operators. The right antenna will make the difference in being able to pilot a craft from 20 miles (32.1 km) away or only a few miles away. Circularly polarized antenna systems or directional antennas can improve signals and cut through potential interference in the airwaves. A quality video receiver that provides an accurate image of what a plane is seeing is also crucial for the successful operation of the aircraft.

CHAPTER SIX

REAL MAKER TALES OF BUILDING UAVs

The maker attitude that people can work together to master technology and come up with solutions and new ideas is evident in a UAV project from the Langley Aerospace Research Student Scholars (LARSS). College students interning at NASA's Langley Research Center worked together to design and build an unmanned aerial vehicle intended to help put out fires in Virginia's Great Dismal Swamp.

Lightning strikes have caused fires in this swamp, and these blazes can burn for months. Locating the fires in these acres of swampland, however, can be difficult. Local fire officials have had to hire pilots to fly over the swamp and scout for the blaze. This can wind up being a costly endeavor.

A UAV offers a less costly solution. The students of LARSS came up with a UAV that could be easily operated by Great Dismal Swamp staff and put into operation within minutes or hours of a possible lightning strike. The potential to pinpoint a fire quickly before it spreads rapidly can bring great savings.

In the Small Unmanned Aerial Vehicle Lab at NASA's Langley Research Center, researcher Mark Motter *(center)* tests a UAV that may one day help pinpoint forest fires.

The team's UAV took the shape of a small plane. They cut the foam framework for the aircraft on a CNC hot wire machine. This is a tool used to cut polystyrene foam. The heat from a wire vaporizes material just in advance of contact, making the desired cuts. To make the aircraft durable, the student team learned how to use protective Kevlar and fiberglass "skins."

They made sure that the UAV could carry a video camera and an infrared camera, which detects heat. The students tried out different motor-propeller combinations, refined the aerodynamic design of their UAV, and installed a navigation system. This is exactly the type of hands-on experience that makerspaces encourage.

ADVANCED TOOLS IN THE MAKERSPACE

While not all makerspaces are equipped with the latest technology, many have state-of-the-art, cutting-edge machinery and materials that can take building UAVs to a whole other level. The Hunt Library Makerspace at North Carolina State University in Raleigh, for example, has two 3-D printers, a laser cutter, and two 3-D scanners. Some makerspaces, like the ones being developed at the Pikes Peak district library in Colorado and the Rochester Makerspace in New York, are also planning on offering 3-D printers, laser cutters, and other sophisticated equipment.

In addition to 3-D printers and laser cutters, Makerhaus provides professional-grade machines for wood and metal work, including sanding, planning, construction of components, parts assembly, cuts, welding, machining, and sheet metal bending.

EMPOWERING STUDENTS THROUGH UAVS

At the Grand Center Arts Academy in St. Louis, Missouri, makerspace manager Andrew Goodin is hoping that the academy's planned UAV project will build community with the sixth through tenth graders at his public charter school. Assuming they will raise the money to build their quadcopter, Goodin pictures multiple students contributing to help build the programming, circuitry, and design. The Grand Center makerspace hopes to equip the quadcopter with features such as a camera, and ultimately the group wants to program it to run an obstacle course.

Students will be involved every step of the way in deciding what is needed to complete the project and how they are going to divide the responsibilities. Students will create timelines for what needs to be done and hold each other accountable. The students will also decide on the troubleshooting process and deal with any challenges and difficulties that arise.

The makerspace at the Grand Center Arts Academy opens an hour before school starts and stays open an hour after school for students to use the resources for school projects or to develop their own projects just for fun. The tools here include a Maker-Bot 3-D printer. One student designed an iPhone case for her mom for Christmas and printed it on the MakerBot.

The makerspace also has a vinyl cutter, which is used mostly for late-end design additions—it allows students to

MakerBot 3D printers, like the one pictured here, are helping bring to life student inventions, from iPhone cases to UAV designs.

add stickers and logos to their project. They also have iPads, laptops, and soldering guns, as well as a pile of cardboard and a collection of other things, all of which might be used to build a maker project. The students will draw on these tools and equipment as they create their quadcopter.

CHAPTER SEVEN

OPPORTUNITIES IN UAV TECHNOLOGY

While it's educational, challenging, and creative to produce UAVs, those who participate in such projects in makerspaces are finding that they are learning very valuable workplace skills as well—even if they're having too much fun to realize it.

As the use of drones continues to grow for military, law enforcement, journalism, and commercial purposes, more professionals are going to be needed to operate, design, and construct such items. Many students and makers who are interested in pursuing aviation as a career are finding that UAVs can lead to a whole new employment pathway.

COLLEGE PROGRAMS TAKE FLIGHT

Sinclair Community College in Dayton, Ohio, has one of the first commercial drone simulator labs in the United States and a program to certify students for employment. They even offer a course online to teach students how to gain approval to fly unmanned aerial systems from the FAA. The classes focus on mission planning, data management, and drone maintenance.

Colleges now offer courses to train students for careers in drone piloting. Here, a pilot at a NASA flight facility guides a UAV designed to track tropical storms, hurricanes, and other weather events.

Other colleges have followed a similar course. The University of North Dakota (UND) has a new program in its department of aviation offering a degree in unmanned-aircraft-systems operations. Like Sinclair Community College, UND also has a drone simulator. Those wanting a degree in this program must complete nineteen lessons or seventy hours on the simulator learning to operate a UAV similar to Boeing's Scan Eagle. The Scan Eagle is a drone that has been in military use since 2004.

The Association for Unmanned Vehicle Systems estimates that projects involving UAVs will employ more than one hundred thousand people by 2025. The association predicts that 90 percent of drone sales will be for agricultural purposes to help farmers with crop dusting, seeding, and scouting crops for health issues.

An operator at the University of California, Davis, tests an unmanned helicopter for agricultural and possible pesticide use, although the FAA currently does not allow pesticide spraying from UAVs.

Schools say that currently most jobs for students with a degree in unmanned-aircraft-systems operations are in the military and law enforcement. Law enforcement officials are interested in using drones to find missing children, rescue lost hikers and others, or track down criminals (spotting their vehicle on a highway, for example). The police department in Starkville, Mississippi, for example, uses a Parrot AR.Drone. Partnering with police in sixteen counties, the police in Grand Forks are training police officers on how to use drones. Police departments in Texas, Florida, and Minnesota have also expressed interest in getting UAVs to assist in their law enforcement efforts.

Many colleges are applying for certificates of authorization to fly drones from the FAA. Both UND and Sinclair are teaching classes about drone law and privacy issues, as well.

WANTED: UAV EXPERTS

In the coming years, the FAA anticipates that ten thousand commercial drones could be flying through U.S. skies. Spending on drone development and production is expected to double, reaching $11.4 billion, according to a report from the Teal Group Corporation, which provides analysis and forecasts for the aerospace and defense industries. Major drone makers today include Northrop Grumman Corporation, General Atomics Aeronautical Systems, and AeroVironment, Inc. Those interested in the military will find that the U.S. Army and Air Force are seeking those interested in piloting UAVs.

THE NEXT STEP AFTER UAVs:
MAKING A REAL PLANE

While UAVs are popular makerspace projects, those who want to really kick it up a notch might consider making their own full-size plane. This is certainly a difficult project that might be beyond the abilities of a young adult, but for those who are passionate about aviation and flying, it's worth finding out about.

A group of makers have started a site called MakerPlane that is intended as an open-source aviation organization. Here people interested in building their own plane can trade information. The goal of the site is to show people how to construct their own personal aircraft of high quality at a reasonable cost using advanced personal manufacturing equipment such as CNC mills (a type of computer-controlled machining) and 3-D printers. The MakerPlane site also includes open source avionics and software to enable state-of-the-art digital flight instruments and display capabilities.

Constructing a self-made airplane is not a new idea. Plenty of websites and organizations provide instructions on how to pull it off and produce a home-built plane (also called amateur-built or kit planes). These aircraft are licensed as "experimental" under FAA rules and regulations. Even putting kits together can be challenging.

The makerspace environment and collaborative attitude should, however, make the process easier for someone who wants to try it.

Those who really want to check out homemade manned aircraft should look into the Experimental Aircraft Association and its annual AirVenture Oshkosh air show in Oshkosh, Wisconsin. Many aviation enthusiasts and makers gather at these shows to demonstrate how their personal aircraft operate.

Another employer of UAV experts is U.S. Immigration and Customs Enforcement. They have been using drones to spot immigrants who try to illegally enter the country as well as drug smugglers who attempt to bring illegal drugs into the U.S. market.

Major corporations are also looking into UAVs for commercial purposes, and they are expected to employ UAV experts to explore their possible use in the near future. Both Federal Express and Amazon have spoken about their interest in delivering packages via drones in the near future.

The maker movement in general is expected to generate jobs and trained employees in the years to come. Not only are makers thinking of innovative business ideas and products, they are empowering people with skills to engineer, build, create, and innovate. Makers like to point out that if it weren't for a similar movement, there might be no Apple or Microsoft.

UAVs, such as this U.S. Air Force Global Hawk drone, are used for national security and surveillance. Some drones are big and powerful enough to deliver heavy equipment.

In 1975, the Homebrew Computer Club brought together electronic enthusiasts and programming fans who wanted to share ideas. Without the Homebrew Computer Club, Steve Wozniak may have never helped create the Apple I computer. This and other similar stories are why many think that some of the most popular new products and successful entrepreneurs will come out of makerspaces.

Steve Bennett has been an active pilot for almost thirty years and a partner of Skyline Flight, an air taxi company that flies passengers on short flights in the Boston area. Bennett sees how the maker movement can foster innovative thinking in the world of aviation and new entrepreneurs. Bennett has been interested in flying since he was a kid and has built his own UAV glider, equipped with a small camera that records flights. Bennett says that makerspaces give people the chance to explore aviation, come up with new ideas, and get the hands-on experience needed to really understand technology.

Bennett led a class that was basically an early version of a makerspace where he asked students to bring in broken toys or appliances. He called it a "take-apart club," and he found a core group of students who really lit up when seeing how the electronics worked. Several of these students went on to engineering school and careers in engineering.

CHAPTER EIGHT

NEW ADVANCES IN UAVS

Ten years ago, no one could predict that UAVs would be flying through the sky and become one of the hottest technological inventions of recent times. The technology used with UAVs is also advancing. The cameras that can be mounted on UAVs have become more sophisticated. The ARGUS-IS (Autonomous Real-Time Ground Ubiquitous Surveillance Imaging System) is essentially a camera system that has the ability to take ultra-high resolution video of a large area. The camera gives an incredibly far range of view of about 4.5 miles (7 km), and the resolution of images comes in super sharp at 1.8 gigapixels.

Some avid makers have been able to figure out how to connect a cell phone to a UAV and use its GPS, camera, two-way long-distance wireless data communications, onboard computing, and storage. They have even figured out how to send certain commands to the UAV rigged with a cell phone via text message— such as "take a photo" or "come home."

USED FOR UTILITY AND OTHER PURSUITS

Other makers have created heavy-lifting quadcopters that can lift the weight of a human being. With this capability, one

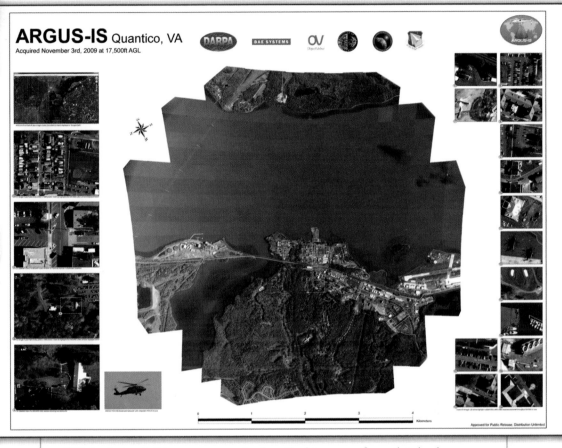

With their ability to transmit detailed images from high above, UAVs can be used to view traffic, track forest fires, search for lost people, observe military operations, and more.

can envision the capabilities to rescue a person in a difficult to reach area, such as possibly lowering a harness and flying a stranded or injured person to safety and medical attention.

One area that has shown the sophisticated uses of UAVs is agriculture. UAVs can be equipped with infrared imagers and other sensors to monitor livestock and crops, detect diseases, and sense plant ripeness. They can distribute poisons to get rid of rats, mice, and other vermin with pinpoint accuracy that reduces harm to the environment.

The robotics team at Queensland University in Australia has shown that a new type of paper airplane can be controlled like a UAV. They have built light paper aircraft with electronics in the fold of the paper, which allows for electronic steering and capturing data. Called Polyplanes, these specially outfitted paper airplanes have been designed to capture atmospheric data in forest fires.

OTHER HIGH-FLYING MAKERSPACE PROJECTS

In addition to radio-controlled planes and quad-copters, these flight-related items are great for makerspace projects.

- **Miniature blimps.** Remote controlled helium blimps can be a fun way to explore UAVs, and they can be equipped with cameras as well.
- **Aerial kite photography.** Also called kite aerial photography, these projects also use FPV cameras that can capture the view from high in the sky.
- **Autogyros.** Similar to helicopters, autogyros use a single propeller to sail through the air. Small radio controlled autogyros and helicopters are both great ways to explore aviation and flight.

In perhaps more juvenile pursuits, one maker on the website DIYDrones.com has posted a video showing how to outfit a hexacopter (with six propellers) to drop water balloons. These may not be the most sophisticated advances in UAV technology, but they do show how creative minds are using these types of aircraft in new ways.

Because UAV experts are in demand, more schools are teaching UAV technology. At Warren County Technical School in New Jersey, student Dan Werbin learns how to assemble a drone.

REGULATING UAVS

As UAVs grow in popularity and use, their regulation may grow, too. Currently, makers who create UAVs do not have to get approval from the Federal Aviation Administration to fly their creations. The FAA says they should be kept no higher than 400 feet (121.9 m) and flown at a sufficient distance away from populated areas, but there are no strict regulations on this. As of this writing, the FAA is said to be in the beginning stages of drafting rules that may govern the flight of UAVs.

Makerspaces are empowering those to see how they can change the world with their ideas. As Apple founder Steve Jobs said, "Life can be much broader once you discover one simple fact, and that is, everything around you that you call life was made up by people that were no smarter than you ... the minute that you understand that you can poke life ... that you can change it, you can mold it ... that's maybe the most important thing."

Arduino (Ardupilot) A single-board microcontroller-based computer often used by hobbyists and makers to create robotics, devices, and gadgets. There is also an Arduino programming language used to make these computers function. Ardupilot is a fully programmable autopilot for a UAV. It is programmed with an Arduino.

circuit A pathway through which electrical current flows. The path starts and ends at the same point, the power supply.

drone An unmanned aerial vehicle, most commonly associated with military and surveillance, that can be flown outside of the pilot's line of sight.

fabrication Making a product from raw materials, such as plastic, metal, rubber, and wood.

first-person view This is a method of piloting a radio-controlled UAV. Also called remote-person view or video piloting, this technique gives an operator on the ground a view from the pilot's seat on the aircraft via an onboard camera that transmits an image to a video monitor on the ground.

global positioning system A navigational system that uses satellites to determine locations on the surface of the earth. A GPS device on a UAV will transmit information back to the pilot to show exactly where the UAV is.

laser cutter A device that cuts through materials in a non-contact process using a laser beam. A combination of heat and pressure creates the cutting action.

LCD A liquid crystal display is an inexpensive low-power display screen. An LCD screen is constructed of a liquid containing crystals that are changed by electric current.

microcontroller A compact microcomputer that may operate a system in a robot, motor vehicle, office machine, medical device, vending machine, home appliance, and other devices.

nano A prefix indicating that something is very small or minute.

open source A computer program or hardware design with free access to source files for the general public to use and even modify from their original designs.

polystyrene Created from ethylene and benzine, this very strong plastic can be injected or molded and makes for a commonly used manufacturing material. Many know polystyrene best in the form of styrofoam.

PVC pipe Polyvinyl chloride pipe is white synthetic thermoplastic pipe used in construction and plumbing and known for its durability and light weight.

quadcopter Also called a quadrocopter, this aerial vehicle is powered by four rotors or propellers.

remote-person view (RPV) Another term for first-person view.

silicone wire Electrical wire insulated with silicone, ideal for making custom-built electrical projects. Silicone is a chemical that does not let water or heat pass through.

telemetry The science and technology of automated measurement and transmission of information through wire, radio signals, or other means. Telemetry systems are key in operating a UAV.

3-D printing A process of making three-dimensional objects from a digital model. Objects are made by laying down successive layers of material.

wattmeter An instrument for measuring electric power (or the supply rate of electrical energy) in watts of any given circuit.

Academy of Model Aeronautics
5161 E. Memorial Drive
Muncie, IN 47302
(800) 435-9262
Website: http://www.modelaircraft.org
This group is dedicated to model aviation enthusiasts, offering free youth membership, publications, educational programs, competitions, and events.

Association of Information Technology Professionals (AITP)
330 N. Wabash Avenue, Suite 2000
Chicago, IL 60611-4267
(800) 224-9371
Website: http://www.aitp.org
This worldwide society of professionals in information technology offers career training, scholarships, news, and social networking opportunities.

Canadian Advanced Technology Alliance (CATA)
207 Bank Street, Suite 416
Ottawa, ON K2P 2N2
Canada
(613) 236-6550
Website: http://www.cata.ca
The largest high-tech association in Canada, CATA is a comprehensive resource of the latest high-tech news in Canada.

International Miniature Aircraft Association
Burr Oak Lane
Salina, KS 67401
(785) 823-5569
Website: http://www.fly-imaa.org
Dedicated to advancing the operation of "large-scale" radio-controlled mode aircraft, this nonprofit supports the non-competitive sport of building and flying large-sized model airplanes throughout the United States and Canada.

Unmanned Systems Canada
P.O. Box 81055
Ottawa, ON K1P 1B1
Canada
(613) 435-0935
Website: http://www.unmannedsystems.ca
This association organizes efforts for public awareness, education, and appreciation for the Canadian unmanned vehicle systems community. The group offers student competitions and scholarships for those interested in the UAV field.

WEBSITES

Due to the changing nature of Internet links, Rosen Publishing has developed an online list of websites related to the subject of this book. This site is updated regularly. Please use this link to access the list:

http://www.rosenlinks.com/MAKER/Unman

Barnhart, Richard, Stephen Hottman, Douglas M. Marshall, and Eric Sharpee. *Introduction to Unmanned Aircraft Systems*. Boca Raton, FL: CRC Press/Taylor & Francis Group, 2011.

Bedson, Colin. *Flying Radio-Controlled Model Aircraft*. Wiltshire, England: Crowood, 2007.

Boxall, John. *Arduino Workshop: A Hands-on Inroduction With 65 Projects*. San Francisco, CA: No Starch Press, 2013.

Doctorow, Cory. *Little Brother*. New York, NY: Macmillan, 2008.

Fahlstrom, Paul. *Introduction to UAV Systems*. Hoboken, NJ: Wiley, 2012.

Frauenfelder, Mark. *The Best of Make* (Make 75 Projects from the pages of MAKE). Sebastapol, CA: Maker Media, 2007.

Goldsworthy, Steve. *Steve Jobs* (Remarkable People). New York, NY: AV2 by Weigl, 2011.

Hamilton, John. UAVs: *Unmanned Aerial Vehicles*. Minneapolis, MN: ABDO Publishing, 2011.

LeMieux, Jerry. *Drone Entrepreneurship: 30 Businesses You Can Start*. Phoenix, AZ: Unmanned Vehicle University Press, 2013.

Mercer, Bobby. *The Flying Machine Book: Build and Launch 35 Rockets, Gliders, Helicopters, Boomerangs, and More* (Science in Motion). Chicago, IL: Chicago Review Press, 2012.

Monk, Simon. *30 Arduino Projects for the Evil Genius*. New York, NY: McGraw-Hill/TAB Electronics: 2010.

Warren, John-David, Josh Adams, and Harold Malle. *Arduino Robotics*. New York, NY: Apress, 2011.

Wesselhoeft, Conrad. *Dirt Bikes, Drones and Other Ways to Fly*. Boston, MA: Houghton Mifflin Harcourt, 2014.

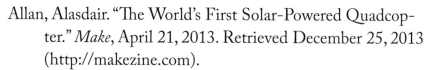

Allan, Alasdair. "The World's First Solar-Powered Quadcopter." *Make*, April 21, 2013. Retrieved December 25, 2013 (http://makezine.com).

Derene, Glenn. "The Art of Flying Your Very Own Drone." *Popular Mechanics*, October 22, 2013. Retrieved December 25, 2013 (http://www.popularmechanics.com).

Handwerk, Brian. "5 Surprising Drone Uses (Besides Pizza Delivery." *National Geographic*, June 6, 2013. Retrieved December 25, 2013 (http://www.nationalgeographic.com).

Federal Aviation Administration. "Fact Sheet: Unmanned Aircraft Systems (UAS)." February 19, 2013. Retrieved December 25, 2013 (http://www.faa.gov).

Lincoln Laboratory. "Student Design Takes Flight: MIT Students Build an Unmanned Aircraft for MIT Lincoln Laboratory Research." December 2010. Retrieved December 25, 2013 (http://www.ll.mit.edu).

Luckerson, Victor. "Majoring in Drones: Higher Ed Embraces Unmanned Aircraft." *Time*, March 18, 2013. Retrieved December 25, 2013 (http://www.time.com).

Maker Faire. "Maker Collaboration: The Air Rocket Glider." Retrieved December 25, 2013 (http://makerfaire.com).

Niquette, Mark. "Ohio Plans Drone to Hunt Lost Kids." Bloomberg, February 19, 2013. Retrieved December 25, 2013 (http://www.bloomberg.com).

Rutherford, Mark. "Unmanned aerial vehicles the size of a cigarette." CNET News, January 19, 2008. Retrieved December 25, 2013 (http://news.cnet.com).

USA Today. "Amazon testing delivery by drone, CEO Bezos says." December 2, 2013. Retrieved December 25, 2013 (http://www.usatoday.com).

ABOUT THE AUTHOR

Don Rauf is passionate about new technology. He was editor of the e-newsletter *Student Health 101*, which featured many cutting-edge interactive elements and videos. He also authored *Killer Lipstick and Other Spy Gadgets*, *Getting the Most Out of Makerspaces to Explore Arduino and Electronics*; and *A Teen's Guide to the Power of Social Networking*. His father was a "tinkerer" and an electrical engineer at IBM. This book is dedicated to him.

PHOTO CREDITS